*The Magician's
Heavenly Chaos*

By Thomas Vaughan

Copyright © 2021 Lamp of Trismegistus. All rights reserved. No part of this publication may be reproduced or transmitted in any form or by any means, electronic or mechanical, including photocopying, recording, or by any information storage and retrieval system, without permission in writing from Lamp of Trismegistus. Reviewers may quote brief passages.

ISBN: 978-1-63118-500-7

Esoteric Classics:
Studies in Alchemy

Other Books in this Series and Related Titles

Aurora of the Philosophers by Paracelsus (978-1-63118-507-6)

Rosicrucian Rules, Secret Signs, Codes and Symbols by various (978-1-63118-488-8)

On the Philadelphian Gold by Philochrysus & Philadelphus (978-1-63118-511-3)

Paracelsus, the Four Elements and Their Spirits by M P Hall (978-1-63118-400-0)

The Stone of the Philosophers by A E Waite (978-1-63118-509-0)

Freher's Process in the Philosophical Work by D A Freher (978-1-63118-484-0)

The Rosicrucian Chemical Marriage by Christian Rosenkreuz (978-1-63118-458-1)

The Alchemical Catechism of Paracelsus by Paracelsus (978-1-63118-513-7)

Alchemy in the Nineteenth Century by Helena P. Blavatsky (978-1-63118-446-8)

Rosicrucians and Speculative Masonry in the Seventeenth Century (978-1-63118-489-5)

Qabbalistic Teachings and the Tree of Life by M P Hall (978-1-63118-482-6)

The Sepher Yetzirah and the Qabalah by M P Hall (978-1-63118-481-9)

The Devil in Love by Jacques Cazotte (978–1–63118–499–4)

Fortune-Telling with Dice by Astra Cielo (978-1-63118-466-6)

History, Analysis and Secret Tradition of the Tarot by Hall &c (978-1-63118-445-1)

Crystal Vision Through Crystal Gazing by Frater Achad (978-1-63118-455-0)

The Golden Verses of Pythagoras: Five Translations (978-1-63118-479-6)

Brothers & Builders by Joseph Fort Newton (978-1-63118-506-9)

Arcane Formulas or Mental Alchemy by W W Atkinson (978-1-63118-459-8)

The Machinery of the Mind by Dion Fortune (978-1-63118-451-2)

The Leadbeater Reader: A Selection of Occult Essays (978-1-63118-483-3)

Audio versions are also available on Audible, Amazon and Apple

Other Books in this Series and Related Titles

On the Cave of the Nymphs in the Odyssey by Thomas Taylor (978-1-63118-505-2)

The Poem of Hashish by A Crowley & C Baudelaire (978-1-63118-484-0)

The Mysteries of Freemasonry & the Druids by M P Hall &c (978-1-63118-444-4)

The Kabbalah of Masonry & Related Writings by E Levi &c (978-1-63118-453-6)

A Collection of Fiction and Essays by Occult Writers on Supernatural and Metaphysical Subjects by various (978–1–63118–510–6)

Clairvoyance and Psychic Abilities by A Besant &c (978-1-63118-403-1)

Cloud Upon the Sanctuary by Waite & K Eckartshausen (978-1-63118-438-3)

The Hymns of Hermes by G. R. S. Mead (978-1-63118-405-5)

The Secrets of Enoch by Enoch (978-1-63118-449-9)

Masonic and Rosicrucian History by M P Hall & H Voorhis (978-1-63118-486-4)

The Sword of Welleran and Other Stories by Lord Dunsany (978-1-63118-501-4)

The Janeites, The Man Who Would Be King and Other Stories of Freemasonry by Rudyard Kipling (978–1–63118–480–2)

Gnosis of the Mind by G. R. S. Mead (978-1-63118-408-6)

The First and Second Gospels of the Infancy of Jesus Christ by Thomas and James (978-1-63118-415-4)

The Life of Pythagoras by Porphyry (978-1-63118-512-0)

Freemasonry & Catholicism by Max Heindel (978-1-63118-508-3)

The Feminine Occult by various authors (978-1-63118-711-7)

The Influence of Pythagoras on Freemasonry and Other Essays (978-1-63118-404-8)

The Path of Light: A Manual of Maha-Yana Buddhism (978-1-63118-471-0)

Tao Te Ching & Commentary by Lao Tzu & C Johnston (978-1-63118-495-6)

Audio versions are also available on Audible, Amazon and Apple

Table of Contents

Introduction...7

COELUM TERRAE

Or *The Magician's Heavenly Chaos*

By Thomas Vaughn...9

INTRODUCTION

The word "esoteric" can be difficult to define. Esotericism in general can be seen less as a system of beliefs and more as a category, which encompasses numerous, different systems of beliefs. It's a bit of juxtaposition, since the word "esoteric" indicates something that few people know about, while the term itself broadly covers numerous philosophies, practices, areas of study and belief systems.

In a greater sense, Esotericism acts as a storehouse for secret knowledge, which is often considered ancient (by *tradition, if not by fact),* passed down from generation to generation, in private. At various times in history, simply possessing the knowledge of some of these subjects, was considered illegal and a jailable offence, if discovered. This usually included such general topics as Alchemy, Pharmacology, Qabalah, Hermeticism, Occultism, Ceremonial Magic, Astrology, Divination, Rosicrucianism and so on. Collectively, these areas of study were often referred to as the esoteric sciences.

Sometimes, the outer garment of a subject isn't esoteric, while what is hidden beneath it, is. As an example, Freemasonry isn't necessarily esoteric by nature (at *least not anymore),* but certain signs, passwords and handshakes given to the candidate during their initiation, are in fact, esoteric, in the sense that they are hidden from the general public.

Today, in the twenty-first century, such topics are readily available at bookstores across the country, and numerous mainsteam publishers offer beginners guides and coffee-table volumes on many of these subjects, intended for mass appeal. Books like *"The Secret"* have turned previously arcane topics into household knowledge. All that being the case, however, it isn't to say that there still aren't buried secrets to uncover, ancient wisdom being ignored and forgotten mysteries to be explored. In fact, it is often that we are only able to further our own studies by standing on the shoulders of these disappearing giants.

Lamp of Trismegistus is doing its part to help preserve humanity's esoteric history by making some of these classics available to those students who are seeking to unearth the knowledge of these ancient colossi.

So, be sure to check other titles from our *Esoteric Classics* series, as well as our *Occult Fiction, Theosophical Classics, Foundations of Freemasonry Series, Supernatural Fiction, Paranormal Research Series, Studies in Buddhism* and our *Christian Apocrypha Series.* You can also download the audio versions of most of these titles from Amazon, Apple or Audible, for learning on the go.

COELUM TERRAE

Or

The Magician's Heavenly Chaos

I have now, Reader, performed my promise and -- according to my *posse* -- proved the antiquity of magic. I am not so much a fool as to expect a general subscription to my endeavours. Every man's *placet* is not the same with mine; but "the die is cast". I have done this much, and he that will overthrow it must know, in the first place, it is his task to do more. There is just one point I can justly bind an adversary to -- that he shall not oppose man to God, heathen romances to Divine Scriptures. He that would foil me must use such weapons as I do, for I have not fed my readers with straw, neither will I be confuted with stubble. In the next place, it is my design to speak something of the Art itself, and this I shall do in rational terms, a form different from the ancients; for I will not stuff my discourse like a wilderness with lions and dragons. To common philosophers that fault is very proper which Quintilian observed in some orators: "The summits of their structures are in evidence; the foundations are hidden." The spires of their Babel are in the clouds, its fundamentals nowhere. They talk indeed of fine things but tell us not upon what grounds. To avoid these flights, I shall in this my *olla* -- for I care not much what I shall call it -- observe this composition. First, I shall speak of that one only thing which is the subject of this Art and the mother of all things. Secondly, I will discourse of that most admirable and more than natural

Medicine which is generated out of this one thing. Lastly -- though with some disorder -- I will discover the means how and by which this Art works upon the subject; but these being the keys which lead to the very *estrado* of Nature, where she sits in full solemnity and receives the visits of the philosophers, I must scatter them in several parts of the discourse. This is all, and here thou must not consider how long or short I shall be but how full the discovery; and truly it shall be such and so much that thou canst not in modesty expect more.

Now then, you that would be what the ancient physicians were, "the health-giving hands of the gods", not quacks and salvos of the pipkin; you that would perform what you publicly profess and make your callings honest and conscionable: attend to the truth without spleen. Remember that prejudice is no religion and by consequence hath no reward. If this Art were damnable you might safely study it notwithstanding, for you have a precept to "prove all things" but to "hold fast that which is good". It is your duty not to be wanting to yourselves; and for my part -- that I may be wanting to none -- thus I begin.

Said the Kabalist: "The building of the Sanctuary which is here below is framed according to that of the Sanctuary which is above." Here we have two worlds, visible and invisible, and two universal Natures, visible and invisible, out of which both those worlds proceeded. The passive universal Nature was made in the image of the active universal one, and the conformity of both worlds or Sanctuaries consists in the original conformity of their principles. There are many Platonics -- and this last century hath afforded them some apish disciples -- who discourse very boldly of the similitudes of inferiors and superiors; but if we thoroughly search their trash it is a pack of small conspiracies -- namely, of the heliotrope and the sun, iron and the lodestone, the wound and the weapon. It is excellent sport to hear how they crow, being roosted on these pitiful particulars, as if they knew the universal magnet which binds this great frame and moves all the members of it to a mutual compassion. This is an humour much like that of Don Quixote, who knew Dulcinea but never saw her. Those students then who would be better instructed must first know there is an universal agent, Who when He was disposed to create had no other pattern or exemplar whereby to frame and mould His creatures but Himself. But having infinite inward ideas or conceptions in Himself, as He conceived so He created: that is to say, He created an outward form answerable to the inward conception or figure of His mind. In the second place, they ought to know there is an universal patient, and this passive Nature was created by the Universal Agent. This general patient is the immediate catholic character of God Himself in His Unity and trinity. In plain terms it is that substance which we commonly call the First Matter. But verily it is to no purpose to know this notion (or) Matter unless we know the thing itself to which the notion relates. We must see it, handle it and by experimental ocular demonstration know the very central invisible essences and properties of it. But of these things hear the most excellent Capnion, who informs his Jew and his Epicure of two catholic natures -- material and spiritual.

One nature (saith he) is such it may be seen with the eyes and felt with the hands, and it is subject to alteration almost in every moment. You must pardon -- as Apuleius saith -- this strange expression, because it makes for the obscurity of the thing. This very nature -- since she may not continue one and the same -- is notwithstanding apprehended of the mind under her such qualification more rightly as she is than as she is not, namely, as the thing itself is in truth -- that is to say, changeable. The other nature or principle of substances is incorruptible, immutable, constant, one and the same forever, and always existent.

Thus he. Now, this changeable nature whereof he speaks is the first, visible, tangible substance that ever God made: it is white in appearance and Paracelsus gives you the reason why: "All things," saith he, "when they first proceed from God are white, but He colours them afterwards according to His pleasure." An example we have in this very matter, which the philosophers call sometimes their Red Magnesia, sometimes their white, by which descriptions they have deceived many men. For in the first preparation the chaos is blood-red, because the Central Sulphur is stirred up and discovered by the Philosophical Fire. In the second it is exceeding white and transparent like the heavens. It is in truth somewhat like common quicksilver, but of a celestial, transcendent brightness, for there is nothing upon earth like it. This fine substance is the child of the elements and it is a most pure sweet virgin, for nothing as yet hath been generated out of her. But if at any time she breeds it is by the fire of Nature, for that is her husband. She is no animal, no vegetable, no mineral, neither is she extracted out of animals, vegetables or minerals, but she is pre-existent to them all, for she is the mother of them. Yet one thing I must say: she is not much short of life, for she is almost animal. Her composition is miraculous and different from all other compounds whatsoever. Gold is not so compact but every sophister concludes it is no simple; but she is so much one that no man believes she is more. She yields to nothing but love, for her end is generation and that was never yet performed by violence. He that knows how to wanton and toy with her, the same shall receive all her treasures. First, she sheds at her nipples a thick, heavy water, but white as any snow: the philosophers call it Virgin's Milk. Secondly, she gives him blood from her very heart: it is a quick, heavenly fire; some improperly call it their sulphur. Thirdly and lastly, she presents him with a secret crystal, of more worth and lustre than the white rock and all her rosials. This is she, and these are her favours: catch her, if you can.

To this character and discovery of my own I shall add some more descriptions, as I find her limned and dressed by her other lovers. Some few -- but such as knew her very well -- have written that she is not only one and three but withal four and five, and this truth is essential. The titles they have bestowed on her are diverse. They call her their Catholic Magnesia and the Sperm of the World out of which all natural things are generated. Her birth -- say they -- is singular and not without a miracle, her complexion heavenly and different from her parents. her body also in some sense is incorruptible and the common elements cannot destroy it, neither will she mix with them essentially. In the outward shape or figure she resembles a stone and yet is no stone, for they call her their White Gum and Water of the Sea, Water of Life, Most Pure and Blessed Water; and yet they mind not water of the clouds or rain water, nor water of the well, nor dew, but a certain thick, permanent, saltish water, that is dry and wets not the hands, a viscous, slimy water generated out of the fatness of the earth. They call her also their twofold Mercury and Azoth, begotten by the influences of two globes, celestial and terrestrial. Moreover, they affirm her to be of that nature that no fire can destroy her, which of all other descriptions is most true, for she is fire herself, having in her a portion of the universal fire of Nature and a secret celestial spirit, which spirit is animated and quickened by God Himself, wherefore also they call her their Most Blessed Stone. Lastly, they say she is a middle nature between thick and thin, neither altogether earthy nor altogether fiery but a mean aerial substance -- to be found everywhere and every time of the year.

This is enough. But that I may speak something myself in plain terms, I say she is a very salt, but extreme soft and somewhat thin and fluid, not so hard, not so thick as common extracted salts, for she is none of them, nor any kind of salt whatsoever that man can make. She is a sperm that Nature herself draws out of the elements without the help of art. Man may find it where Nature leaves it; it is not of his office to make the sperm, nor to extract it. It is already made and wants nothing but a matrix and heat convenient for generation. Now should you consider with yourselves where Nature leaves the seed, and yet many are so dull they know not how to work when they are told what they must do. We see in animal generations the sperm parts not from both the parents, for it remains with the female, where it is perfected. In the great world, though all the elements contribute to the composure of the sperm yet the sperm parts not from all the elements but remains with the earth or with the water though more immediately with the one than with the other. Let not your thoughts feed now on the phlegmatic, indigested vomits of Aristotle; look on the green, youthful and flowery bosom of the earth. Consider what a vast universal receptacle this element is. The stars and planets overlook her and -- though they may not descend hither themselves -- they shed down their golden locks, like so many bracelets and tokens of love. The sun is perpetually busy, brings his fire round her, as if he would sublime something from her bosom and rob her of some secret, enclosed jewel. Is there anything lost since the creation? Wouldst thou know his very bed and his pillow? It is the earth. How many cities, dost thou think, have perished with the sword? How many by earthquakes? And how many by the deluge? Thou dost perhaps desire to know where they are at this present: believe it, they have one common sepulchre. What was once their mother is now their tomb. All things return to that place from whence they came, and that very place is earth. If thou hast but leisure, run over the alphabet of Nature; examine every letter -- I mean every particular creature -- in her book. What becomes of her grass, her corn, her herbs, her flowers? True it is, both man and beast do use them, but this only by the way, for they rest not till they come to earth again. In this element they had their first and in this will they have their last station. Think -- if other vanities will give thee leave -- on all those generations that went before thee and anticipate all those that shall come after thee. Where are those beauties the times past have produced and what will become of those that shall appear in future ages? They will all to the same dust; they have one common house; and there is no family so numerous as that of the grave. Do but look on the daily sports of Nature, her clouds and mists, the scene and pageantry of the air. Even these momentary things retreat to the closet of the earth. If the sun makes her dry she can drink as fast; what gets up in clouds comes down in water; the earth swallows up all and like that philosophical dragon eats her own tail. The wise poets saw this and in their mystical language called the earth Saturn, telling us withal she did feed on her own children. Verily, there is more truth in their stately verse than in Aristotle's dull prose, for he was a blind beast and malice made him so.

But to proceed a little further with you, I wish you to concoct what you read, to dwell a little upon earth, not to fly up presently and admire the meteors of your own brains. The earth, you know, in the winter-time is a dull, dark, dead thing -- a contemptible, frozen, phlegmatic lump. But towards the spring and fomentations of the sun what rare pearls are there in this dung-hill, what glorious colours and tinctures doth she discover! A pure, eternal green overspreads her, and this attended with innumerable other beauties -- roses red and white, golden lilies, azure violets, the bleeding hyacinths, with their several celestial odours and spices. If you will be advised by me, learn from whence the earth hath these invisible treasures, this annual flora, which appears not without the compliments of the sun. Behold, I will tell you as plainly as I may. There are in the world two extremes -- matter and spirit. One of these, I can assure you, is earth. The influences of the spirit animate and quicken the matter, and in the material extreme the seed of the spirit is to be found. In middle natures

-- as fire, air, and water -- this seed stays not, for they are but *dispenseros* or *media*, which convey it from one extreme to the other, from the spirit to the matter -- that is, the earth. But stay, my friend; this intelligence hath somewhat stirred you, and how you come on so furiously, as if you would rifle the cabinet. Give me leave to put you back. I mind not this common, feculent, impure earth; that falls not within my discourse, but as it makes for your manuduction. That which I speak of is a mystery: it is *coelum terrae* and *terrae coeli*, not this dirt and dust but a most secret, celestial, invisible earth.

Raymund Lully, in his *Compendium of Alchemy*, calls the principles of art magic "certain fugitive spirits, condensed in the air, in the shape of diverse monsters, beasts and men, which move like clouds hither and thither". As for the sense of our Spaniard, I refer it to his readers; let them make the most of it.

This is true; as the air and all the volatile substances in it are restless, even so is it with the First Matter. The eye of man never saw her twice under one and the same shape; but as clouds driven by the wind are forced to this and that figure -- but cannot possibly retain one constant form -- so is she persecuted by the fire of Nature. For this fire and this water are like two lovers: they no sooner meet but presently they play and toy, and this game will not over till some new baby is generated. I have oftentimes admired their subtle perpetual motion, for at all time and in all places these two are busy, which occasioned that notable sentence of Trismegistus', that action was the life of God. But most excellent and magisterial is that oracle of Marcus Antoninus, who in his discourse to himself speaks indeed things worthy of himself. "The nature," saith he, "of the universe delights not in anything so much as to alter all things and then to make the like again." This is her tick-tack: she plays one game, to begin another. The Matter is placed before her like a piece of wax, and she shapes it to all forms and figures. Now she makes a bird, now a beast, now a flower, then a frog, and she is pleased with her own magical performances as men are with their own fancies. Hence she is called of Orpheus "the mother that makes many things and ordains strange shapes or figures". Neither doth she as some sinful parents do, who -- having their pleasure -- care not for their child. She loves them still after she hath made them, hath an eye over them all and provides even for her sparrows. 'Tis strange to consider that she works as well privately as publicly, not only in gardens, where ladies may smell her perfumes, but in remote solitudes and deserts. The truth is she seeks not to please others so much as herself, wherefore many of her works -- and those the choicest -- never come to light.

    We see little children, who are newly come from under her hand, will be dabbling in dirt and water, and other idle sports affected by none but themselves. The reason is they are not as yet captivated, which makes them seek their own pleasures. But when they come to age then love or profit makes them square their actions according to other men's desires. Some cockney claps his revenue on his back, but his gallantry is spoiled if his mistress doth not observe it. Another fights, but this victory is lost if it be not printed; it is the world must hear of his valour. Now, Nature is a free spirit that seeks no applause; she observes none more than herself but is pleased with her own magic, as philosophers are with their secret philosophy. Hence it is that we find her busy not only in the pots of the balconies but in wildernesses and ruinous places, where no eyes observe her but the stars and planets. In a word, wheresoever the fire of Nature finds the Virgin Mercury there hath he found his love, and there will they both fall to their husbandry, a pleasure not subject to surfeits, for it still presents new varieties.

It is reported of Mark Antony, a famous but unfortunate Roman, how he sent his agent over the world to copy all the handsome faces, that amongst so many excellent features he might select for himself the most pleasing piece. Truly Nature is much of this strain, for she hath infinite beauteous patterns in herself, and all these she would gladly see beyond herself, which she cannot do without the Matter -- for that is her glass. This makes her generate perpetually and imprint her conceptions in the Matter, communicating life to it and figuring it according to her imagination. By this practice she placeth her fancy or idea beyond herself, or, as the Peripatetics say, beyond the Divine Mind, namely, in the Matter. But the ideas being innumerable and withal different, the pleasures of the agent are maintained by their variety or -- to speak more properly -- by his own fruitfulness, for amongst all the beauties the world affords there are not two that are altogether the same.

Much might be spoken in this place concerning beauty, what it is, from whence it came, and how it may be defaced, not only in the outward figure but in the inward idea and lost for ever in both worlds. But these pretty shuttles I am no way acquainted with: I have no mistress but Nature, wherefore I shall leave the fine ladies to fine lads and speak of my simple

AElia Laelia

It was scarce day when all alone
I saw Hyanthe and her throne.
In fresh green damask she was dressed
And o'er a sapphire globe did rest.
This slippery sphere when I did see,
Fortune, I thought it had been thee.
But when I saw she did present
A majesty more permanent
I thought my cares not lost if I
Should finish my discovery.

Sleepy she look'd to my first sight,
As if she had watch'd all the night,
And underneath her hand was spread
The white supporter of her head.
But at my second, studied view
I could perceive a silent dew
Steal down her cheeks, lest it should stain
Those cheeks where only smiles should reign.
The tears stream'd down for haste and all
In chains of liquid pearl did fall.
Fair sorrows -- and more dear than joys,
Which are but empty airs and noise --
Your drops present a richer prize,
For they are something like her eyes.

Pretty white fool, why hast thou been
Sullied with tears and not with sin?
'Tis true thy tears, like polished skies,
Are the bright rosials of thy eyes;
But such strange fates do them attend
As if thy woes would never end.
From drops to sighs they turn and then
Those sighs return to drops again;
But whiles the silver torrent seeks
Those flowers that watch it in thy cheeks
The white and red Hyanthe wears
Turn to rose-water all her tears.

Have you beheld a flame that springs
From incense when sweet curled rings
Of smoke attend her last weak fires,
And she all in perfumes expires?
So did Hyanthe. Here -- said she --
Let not this vial part from thee.
It holds my heart, though now 'tis spill'd
And into waters all distill'd.
'Tis constant still. Trust not false smiles:
Who smiles and weeps not she beguiles.
Nay, trust not tears: false are the few;
Those tears are many that are true.
Trust me and take the better choice:
Who hath my tears can want no joys.

I know some sophisters of the Heptarchy -- I mean those whose learning is all noise, in which sense even pyannets and paraquitoes are philosophical -- will conclude this all bait and poetry; that we are pleasing, not positive, and cheat even the reader's discretion. To prevent such impotent calumnies, and to spend a little more of our secret light upon the well-disposed student, I shall in this place produce the testimonies of some able philosophers concerning the First Matter itself, as it is naturally found before any alteration by art. And here verily the reader may discover the mark. It is most easily done, if he will but eye the flights of my verse or follow the more grave pace of their prose. The first I shall cite is Arnoldus de Nova, an absolute perfect master of the Art. He describes the Philosophical Chaos in these plain terms:

It is (saith he) a stone and no stone, spirit, soul, and body; which if thou dissolvest, it will be dissolved; and if thou dost coagulate it, it will be coagulated; and if thou dost make it fly, it will fly; for it is volatile or flying and clear as a tear. Afterwards it is made citrine, then saltish; but without shoots or crystals, and no man may touch it with his tongue. Behold, I have described it truly to thee, but I have not named it. Now I will name it; and I say that if thou sayest it is water thou dost say the truth; and if thou sayest it is not water thou dost lie. Be not therefore deceived with manifold descriptions and operations, for it is but one thing, to which nothing extraneous may be added.

Thus Arnoldus, and he borrowed this from the Turba. Let us now hear his disciple Raymund Lully, who, speaking very enviously and obscurely of seven metallic principles, describes the third -- wherein four of the seven are included -- in these words. Saith he:

The third principle is a clear, compounded water, and it is the next substance in complexion to quicksilver. It is found running and flowing upon the earth. This quicksilver is generated in every compound out of the substance of the air, and therefore the moisture of it is extreme heavy.

To these I will add Albertus Magnus, whose suffrage in this kind of learning is like the stylanx to gold, for he had thoroughly searched it and knew very well what part of it would abide the test. In plain English saith he:

The Mercury of the wise men is a watery element cold and moist. This is their Permanent Water, the spirit of the body, the unctuous vapour, the blessed water, the virtuous water, the water of the wise men, the philosopher's vinegar, the mineral water, the dew of heavenly grace, the virgin's milk, the bodily Mercury; and with other numberless names it is named in the books of the philosophers; which names truly -- though they are divers notwithstanding -- always signify one and the same thing, namely, the Mercury of the wise men. Out of this Mercury alone all the virtue of the Art is extracted and -- according to its nature -- the Tincture, both red and white.

To this agrees Rachaidibi, the Persian. "The sperm or First Matter," saith he, "of the stone is outwardly cold and moist but inwardly hot and dry." All which is confirmed by Rhodian, another instructor, it seems, of Kanid, King of Persia. His words are these:

The sperm is white and liquid, afterwards red. This sperm is the Flying Stone, and it is aerial and volatile, cold and moist, hot and dry.

To these subscribes the author of that excellent tract entitled *The Book of the Three Words*.

This (saith he) is the Book of Three Words, meaning thereby Three Principles; the Book of the Precious Stone, which is a body aerial and volatile, cold and moist, watery and adustive; and in it is heat and drought, coldness and moisture, one virtue inwardly, the other outwardly.

Belus the philosopher, in that famous and most classic Synod of Arisleus, inverts the order to conceal the practice; but if rightly understood he speaks to the same purpose.

Amongst all great philosophers (saith he) it is magisterial that our Stone is no stone; but amongst ignorants it is ridiculous and incredible. For who will believe that water can be made a stone and a stone water, nothing being more different than these two? And yet in very truth it is so. For this very Permanent Water is the Stone; but whiles it is water it is no stone.

But in this sense the ancient Hermes abounds and almost discovers too much.

Know (saith he), you that are children of the wise: the separation of the ancient philosophers was performed upon water, which separation divides the water into four other substances.

There is extant a very learned author who hath written something to this purpose, and that more openly than any whom we have formerly cited.

As the world (saith he) was generated out of that Water upon which the Spirit of God did move, all things proceeding thence, both celestial and terrestrial, so this chaos is generated out of a certain Water that is not common, not out of dew nor air condensed in the caverns of the earth, or artificially in the receiver; not out of water drawn out of the sea, fountains, pits, or rivers; but out of a certain tortured water that hath suffered some alteration. Obvious it is to all but known to very few. This water hath all in it that is necessary to the perfection of the work, without any extrinsical addition.

I could produce a thousand authors more, but that were tedious. I shall conclude with one of the Rosy Brothers, whose testimony is equivalent to the best of these, but his instruction far more excellent. His discourse of the First Matter is somewhat large, and to avoid prolixity I shall forbear the Latin, but I will give thee his sense in punctual, plain English.

I am a goddess (saith he, speaking in the person of Nature), for beauty and extraction famous, born out of our own proper sea which compasseth the whole earth and is ever restless. Out of my breasts I pour forth milk and blood: boil these two till they are turned into silver and gold. O most excellent subject, out of which all things in this world are generated, though at the first sight thou art poison, adorned with the name of the Flying Eagle. Thou are the First Matter, the seed of Divine Benediction, in whose body there is heat and rain, which notwithstanding are hidden from the wicked, because of thy habit and virgin vestures which are scattered over all the world. Thy parents are the sun and moon; in thee there is water and wine, gold also and silver upon earth, that mortal man may rejoice. After this matter God sends us His blessing and wisdom with rain and the beams of the sun, to the eternal glory of His Name. But consider, O man, what things God bestows upon thee by this means. Torture the Eagle till she weeps and the Lion be weakened and bleed to death. The blood of this Lion, incorporated with the tears of the Eagle, is the treasure of the earth. These creatures use to devour and kill one another, but notwithstanding their love is mutual, and they put on the property and nature of a Salamander, which if it remains in the fire without any detriment it cures all the diseases of men, beasts, and metals. After that the ancient philosophers had perfectly understood this subject they diligently sought in this mystery for the centre of the middlemost tree in the Terrestrial Paradise, entering in by five litigious gates. The first gate was the knowledge of the True Matter, and here arose the first and that a most bitter conflict. The second was the preparation by which this Matter was to be prepared, that they might obtain the embers of the Eagle and the blood of the Lion. At this gate there is a most sharp fight, for it produceth water and blood and a spiritual, bright body. The third gate is the fire which conduceth to the maturity of the Medicine. The fourth gate is that of multiplication and augmentation, in which proportions and weight are necessary. The fifth and last gate is projection. But most glorious, full rich and high is he who attains to the fourth gate, for he hath got an universal Medicine for all diseases. This is that great character of the Book of Nature out of which her whole alphabet doth arise. The fifth gate serves only for metals. This mystery, existing from the foundation of the world and the creation of Adam, is of all others the most ancient, a knowledge which God Almighty -- by His Word -- breathed into Nature, a miraculous power, the blessed fire of life, the transparent carbuncle and red gold of the wise men, and the Divine Benediction of this life. But his mystery, because of the malice and wickedness of men, is given only to few, notwithstanding it lives and moves every day in the sight of the whole world, as it appears by the following parable.

I am a poisonous dragon, present everywhere and to be had for nothing. My water and my fire dissolve and compound. Out of my body thou shalt draw the Green and the Red Lion; but if thou dost not exactly know me thou wilt -- with my fire -- destroy thy five senses. A most pernicious, quick poison comes out of my nostrils which hath been the destruction of many. Separate therefore the thick from the thin artificially, unless thou dost delight in extreme poverty. I give thee faculties both male and female and the powers both of heaven and earth. The mysteries of my art are to be performed magnanimously and with great courage if thou wouldst have me overcome the violence of the fire, in which attempt many have lost both their labour and their substance. I am the egg of Nature known only to the wise such as are pious and modest, who make of me a little world. Ordained I was by the Almighty God for men, but -- though many desire me -- I am given only to few that they may relieve the poor with my treasures and not set their minds on gold that perisheth. I am called of the philosophers Mercury: my husband is gold philosophical. I am the old dragon that is present everywhere on the face of the earth. I am father and mother, youthful and ancient, weak and yet most strong, life and death, visible and invisible, hard and soft, descending to the earth and ascending to the heavens, most high and most low, light and heavy. In me the order of Nature is oftentimes inverted -- in colour, number, weight, and measure. I have in me the light of Nature; I am dark and bright; I spring from the earth and I come out of heaven; I am well known and yet a mere nothing; all colours shine in me and all metals by the beams of the sun. I am the Carbuncle of the Sun, a most noble, clarified earth, by which thou mayst turn copper, iron, tin, and lead into most pure gold.

Now, gentlemen, you may see which way the philosophers move: they commend their Secret Water and I admire the tears of Hyanthe. There is something in the fancy besides poetry, for my mistress is very philosophical and in her love a pure platonic. But now I think upon it, how many rivals shall I procure by this discourse? Every reader will fall to and some fine thing may break her heart with nonsense. This love indeed were mere luck; but for my part I dare trust her, and lest any man should mistake her for some things formerly named I will tell you truly what she is. She is not any known water whatsoever but a secret spermatic moisture, or rather the Venus that yields that moisture. Therefore do not you imagine that she is any crude, phlegmatic, thin water, for she is a fat, thick, heavy, slimy humidity. But let you should think I am grown jealous and would not trust you with my mistress, Arnoldus de Villa Nova shall speak for me: hear him.

> *I tell thee further (saith he) that we could not possibly find,*
> *neither could the philosophers find before us, anything that would persist*
> *in the fire but only the unctuous humidity. A watery humidity we see will*
> *easily vapour away, and the earth remains behind, and the parts are*
> *therefore separated because their composition is not natural. But if we*
> *consider those humidities which are hardly separated from those parts*
> *which are natural to them, we find not any such but the unctuous, viscous*
> *humidities.*

It will be expected perhaps by some flint and antimony doctors -- who make their philosophical contrition with a hammer -- that I should discover thing outright and not suffer this strange bird-lime to hold their pride by the plumes. To these I say it is Water of Silver, which some have called Water of the Moon; but 'tis Mercury of the Sun, and partly of Saturn, for it is extracted from these three metals and without them it can never be made. Now they may unriddle and tell me what it is, for it is truth -- if they can understand it.

To the ingenuous and modest reader I have something else to reply, and I believe it will sufficiently excuse me. Raymund Lully -- a man who had been in the centre of Nature and without all question understood a great part of the Divine Will -- gives me a most terrible charge not to prostitute these principles. Saith he:

> *I swear to thee upon my soul that thou art damned if thou shouldst*
> *reveal these things. For every good thing proceeds from God and to Him*
> *only is due. Wherefore thou shalt reserve and keep that secret which God*

only should reveal, and thou shalt affirm thou dost justly keep back those things whose revelation belongs to His honour. For if thou shouldst reveal that in a few words which God hath been forming a long time, thou shouldst be condemned in the great day of judgement as a traitor to the majesty of God, neither should thy treason be forgiven thee. For the revelation of such things belongs to God and not to man.

So said the wise Raymund.

Now, for my part, I have always honoured the magicians, their philosophy being both rational and majestic, dwelling not upon notions but effects, and those such as confirm both the wisdom and the power of the Creator. When I was a mere errant in their books, and understood them not, I did believe them. Time rewarded my faith and paid my credulity with knowledge. In the interim I suffered many bitter calumnies, and this by some envious adversaries who had nothing of a scholar but their gowns and a little language for vent to their nonsense. But these could not remove me; with a Spartan patience I concocted my injuries and found at last that Nature was magical, not peripatetical. I have no reason then to distrust them in spiritual things, whom I have found so orthodox and faithful even in natural mysteries. I do believe Raymund, and in order to that faith I provide for my salvation. I will not discover, that I may not be condemned. But if this will not satisfy thee -- whoever thou art -- let me whisper thee a word in the ear, and afterwards do thou proclaim it on the housetop. Dost thou know from whom and how that sperm or seed which men for want of a better name call the First Matter proceeded? A certain illuminatee -- and in his days a member of that Society which some painted buzzard use to laugh at -- writes thus:

God (saith he), incomparably good and great, out of nothing created something; but that something was made one thing, in which all things were contained, creatures both celestial and terrestrial.

nihil quo ad nos -- nothing that we perfectly know. It is nothing, as Dionysius saith: it is nothing that was created or of those things that are and nothing of that which thou dost call nothing -- that is, of those things that are not, in thy empty, destructive sense.

But, by your leave, it is the True Thing, of Whom we can affirm nothing. It is that Transcendent Essence Whose theology is negative and was known to the primitive Church but is lost in these our days. That is that nothing of Cornelius Agrippa, and in this nothing when he was tired with human things – I mean human sciences -- he did at last rest. "To know nothing is the happiest life." True indeed, for to know this nothing is life eternal. Learn, then, to understand that magical axiom "the visible was formed form the invisible", for all visibles came out of the invisible God, for He is the well-spring whence all things flow, and the creation was a certain stupendous birth or delivery. This fine Virgin Water, or chaos, was the Second Nature from God Himself and -- if I may say so -- the child of the Blessed Trinity. What doctor, then, is he whose hands are fit to touch that subject upon which God Himself, when He works, lays His own Spirit? For verily so we read: "The Spirit of God moved upon the face of the water."

And can it be expected, then, that I should prostitute this mystery to all hands whatsoever, that I should proclaim it and cry it as they cry oysters? Verily these considerations, with some other which I will not for all the world put to paper, have made me almost displease my dearest friends, to whom, notwithstanding, I owe a better satisfaction. Had it been my fortune barely to know this Matter, as most men do, I had perhaps been less careful of it; but I have been instructed in all the secret circumstances thereof, which few upon earth understand. I speak not for any ostentation, but I speak a truth which my conscience knows very well. Let me, then, Reader, request thy patience, for I shall leave this discovery to God, Who -- if it be His blessed will -- can call unto thee and say: Here it is and thus I work it.

I had not spoken all this in my own defence had I not been assaulted -- as it were -- in this very point and told to my face I was bound to discover all that I knew, for this age looks for dreams and revelations as the train to their invisible righteousness. I have now sufficiently discoursed of the Matter, and if it be not thy fortune to find it by what is here written, yet thou canst not be deceived by what I have said, for I have purposely avoided all those terms which might make thee mistake any common salts, stones, or minerals for it. I advise thee withal to beware of all vegetables and animals: avoid them and every part of them whatsoever. I speak this because some ignorant, sluttish broilers are of opinion that man's blood is the true subject. But, alas, is man's blood in the bowels of the earth, that metals should be generated out of it? Or was the world and all that is therein made out of man's blood as of their first matter? Surely no such thing. The First Matter was existent before man and all other creatures whatsoever, for she is the mother of them all. They were made of the First Matter, and not the First Matter of them. Take heed, then: let not any man deceive thee. It is totally impossible to reduce any particular to the First Matter or to a sperm without our Mercury, and being so reduced it is not universal but the particular sperm of its own species, and works not any effects but what are agreeable to the nature of that species: for God hath sealed it with a particular idea. Let them alone, then, who practise upon man's blood in their chemical stoves and athanors, or, as Sendivogius hath it, *in fornaculis mirabilibus*. They will deplore their error at last and sit without sackcloth in the ashes of their compositions.

But I have done. I will now speak something of generation and the ways of it, that the process of the philosophers upon this matter may be the better understood. You must know that Nature hath two extremes and between them a middle substance, which elsewhere we have called the middle nature. Example enough we have in creation. The first extreme was that cloud or darkness whereof we have spoken formerly. Some call it the remote matter and the invisible chaos, but very improperly, for it was not invisible. This is the Jewish *Soph* outwardly, and it is the same with that Orphic night:

"O Night, thou black nurse of the golden stars."

Out of this darkness all things that are in this world came, as out of their fountain or matrix. Hence that position of all famous poets and philosophers -- that "all things were brought forth out of night". The middle substance is the Water into which that night or darkness was condensed, and the creatures framed out of the water made up the other extreme. But the magicians, when they speak strictly, will not allow of this other extreme, because Nature does not stay here: wherefore their philosophy runs thus. Man -- say they -- in his natural state is in the mean creation, from which he must recede to one of two extremes -- either to corruption, as commonly all men do, for they die and moulder away in their graves; or else to a spiritual, glorified condition, like Enoch and Elijah, who were translated. And this -- they say -- is a true extreme, for after it there is no alteration. Now, the magicians, reasoning with themselves why the mean creation should be subject to corruption, concluded the cause and original of this disease to be in the chaos itself, for even that was corrupted and cursed upon the Fall of man. But examining things further they found that Nature in her generations did only concoct the chaos with a gentle heat. She did not separate the parts and purify each of them by itself; but the purities and impurities of the sperm remained together in all her productions, and this domestic enemy prevailing at last occasioned the death of the compound. Hence they wisely gathered that to minister vegetables, animals or minerals for physic was a mere madness, for even these also had their own impurities and diseases, and required some medicine to cleanse them. Upon this *adviso* they resolved -- God without all question being their guide -- to practice on the chaos itself. They opened it, purified it, united what they had formerly separated and fed it with a twofold fire, thick and thin, till they brought it to the immortal extreme and made it a spiritual, heavenly body. This was their physic, this was their magic. In this performance they saw the image of that face which Zoroaster calls the pre-existent countenance of the Triad. They perfectly knew the *Secunda* which contains all things in her naturally, as God contains all things in Himself spiritually. They saw that the life of all things here below was a thick fire, or fire imprisoned and incorporated in a certain incombustible, aerial moisture. They found, moreover, that this moisture was originally derived from heaven, and in this sense heaven is styled in Oracles: "Fire, derivation of fire and food of fire."

In a word, they saw with their eyes that Nature was male and female, as the Kabalists express it: a certain fire of a most deep red colour, working on a most white, heavy, salacious water, which water also is fire inwardly, but outwardly very cold. By this practice it was manifested unto them that God Himself was Fire, according to that of Eximidius in *Turba*: "The beginning of all things," saith he, "is a certain nature, and that eternal and infinite, cherishing and heating all things". The truth is, life -- which is nothing else but light -- proceeded originally from God and did apply to the chaos, which is elegantly called by Zoroaster "the fountain of fountains and of all fountains, the matrix containing all things." We see by experience that all individuals live not only by their heat, but they are preserved by the outward universal heat which is the life of the great world. Even so truly the great world itself lives not altogether by that heat which God hath enclosed in the parts thereof, but it is preserved by the circumfused, influent heat of the Deity. For above the heavens God is manifested like an infinite burning world of light and fire, so that He overlooks all that He hath made and the whole fabric stands in His heat and light, as a man stands here on earth in the sunshine. I say then that the God of Nature employs Himself in a perpetual coction, and this not only to generate but to preserve that which hath been generated; for His spirit and heat coagulate that which is thin, rarefy that which is too gross, quicken the dead parts and cherish the cold. There is indeed one operation of heat whose method is vital and far more mysterious than the rest; they that have use for it must study it.

I have for my part spoken all that I intend to speak, and though my book may prove fruitless to many, because not understood, yet some few may be of that spirit as to comprehend it. "Spacious flame of spacious mind," said the great Chaldean. But because I will not leave thee without some satisfaction, I advise thee to take the Moon of the firmament, which is a middle nature, and place her so that every part of her may be in two elements at one and the same time. These elements also must equally attend the body, not one further off, not one nearer than the other. In the regulating of these two there is a twofold geometry to be observed -- natural and artificial. But I may speak no more.

The true furnace is a little simple shell; thou mayest easily carry it in one of thy hands. The glass is one and no more; but some philosophers have used two, and so mayst thou. As for the work itself, it is no way troublesome; a lady may read the *Arcadia* and at the same time attend this philosophy without disturbing her fancy. For my part, I think women are fitter for it than men, for in such things they are more neat and patient, being used to a small chemistry of sack-possets and other finical sugar-sops. Concerning the effects of this medicine I shall not speak anything at this time. He that desires to know them let him read the *Revelation* of Paracelsus, a discourse altogether incomparable and in very truth miraculous. And here without any partiality I shall give my judgment of honest Hohenheim. I find in the rest of his works, and especially where he falls on the Stone, a great many false processes, but his doctrine of it in general is very sound. The truth is he had some pride to the justice of his spleen, and in many places he hath erred of purpose, not caring what bones he threw before the schoolmen, for he was a pilot of Guadalcanar and sailed sometimes in his *rio de la recriation*.

But I had almost forgot to tell thee that which is all in all, and it is the greatest difficulty in all the art -- namely, the fire. It is a close, airy, circular, bright fire: the philosophers call it their sun and the glass must stand in the shade. It makes not the Matter to vapour -- no, not so much as to sweat. It digests only with a still, piercing, vital heat. It is continual and therefore at last alters the chaos and corrupts it. The proportion and regimen of it is very scrupulous, but the best rule to know it by is that of the *Synod*: "Let not the bird fly before the fowler." Make it sit while you give fire, and then you are sure of your prey. For a close I must tell thee the philosophers call this fire their bath, but it is a bath of Nature, not an artificial one; for it is not any kind of water but a certain subtle, temperate moisture which compasseth the glass and feeds their sun or fire. In a word, without this bath nothing in the world is generated. Now, that thou mayst the better understand what degree of fire is requisite for the work, consider the generation of man, or any other creature whatsoever. It is not kitchen fire nor fever that works upon the sperm in the womb, but a most temperate, moist, natural heat which proceeds from the very life of the mother. It is just so here. Our Matter is a most delicate substance and tender, like the animal sperm, for it is almost a living thing. Nay, in very truth, it hath some small portion of life, for Nature doth produce some animals out of it. For this very reason the least violence destroys it and prevents all generation; for if it be overheated but for some few minutes the white and red sulphurs will never essentially unite and coagulate. On the contrary, if it takes cold but for half and hour -- the work being once well begun -- it will never sort to any good purpose. I speak out of my own experience, for I have -- as they phrase it -- given myself a box on the ear, and that twice or thrice, out of a certain confident negligence, expecting that which I knew well enough could never be.

Nature moves not by the theory of men but by their practice, and surely wit and reason can perform no miracles unless the hands supply them. Be sure then to know this fire in the first place, and accordingly be sure to make use of it. But for thy better security I will describe it to thee once more. It is a dry, vaporous, humid fire; it goes round about the glass and is both equal and continual. It is restless, and some have called it the white philosophical coal. It is in itself natural, but the preparation of it is artificial. It is a heat of the dead, wherefore some call it their unnatural, necromantic fire. It is no part of the matter, neither is it taken out of it; but it is an external fire and serves only to stir up and strengthen the inward oppressed fire of the chaos. But let us hear Nature herself, for thus she speaks in the serious romance of Mehung.

> *After putrefaction succeeds generation and that because of the inward, incombustible Sulphur that heats or thickens the coldness and crudities of the Quicksilver, which suffers so much thereby that at last it is united to the Sulphur and made one body therewith. All this -- namely, fire, air, and water -- is contained in one vessel. In their earthly vessel -- that is, in their gross body or composition -- I take them, and then I leave them in one alembic, where I concoct, dissolve and sublime them without the help of hammer, tongs or fire; without coals, smoke, fire or bath; or the alembics of the sophisters. For I have my heavenly fire, which excites or stirs up the elemental one, according as the matter desires a becoming agreeable form.*

Now, Nature everywhere is one and the same, wherefore she reads the same lesson to Madathan, who, thinking in his ignorance to make the Stone without dissolution, receives from her this check. "Dost thou think," says she, "to eat oysters, shells and all? Ought they not first to be opened and prepared by the most ancient cook of the planets?" With these agrees the excellent Flamel, who, speaking of the solar and lunar Mercury -- and the plantation of the one in the other, hath these words: "Take them therefore," saith he, "and cherish them over a fire in thy alembic. But it must not be a fire of coals, nor of any wood, but a bright shining fire, like the Sun itself, whose heat must never be excessive but always of one and the same degree." This is enough and too much, for the secret in itself is not great but the consequences of it are so -- which made the philosophers hide it. Thus, Reader, thou hast the outward agent most fully and faithfully described. It is in truth a very simple mystery and -- if I should tell it openly -- ridiculous.

Howsoever, by this and not without it did the magicians unlock the chaos; and certainly it is no news that an iron key should open a treasury of gold.

In this universal subject they found the natures of all particulars, and this is signified to us by that maxim: "Let him who is not familiar with Proteus have recourse to Pan." This Pan is their chaos or Mercury, which expounds Proteus -- namely, the particular creatures, commonly called individuals. For Pan transforms himself into a Proteus, that is, into all varieties of species, into animals, vegetables, and minerals. For out of the Universal Nature or First Matter all these are made and Pan hath their properties in himself. Hence it is that Mercury is called the Interpreter or Expositor of inferiors and superiors, under which notion the ancient Orpheus invokes him: "Hear me, O Mercury, thou messenger of Jove and son of Maia, the Expositor of all things." Now, for the birth of this Mercury and the place of it I find but few philosophers that mention it. Zoroaster points at it, and that very obscurely, where he speaks of his Lynges or the Ideas in these words: "Their multitudes leap upward, ascending to those shining worlds wherein are the three heights, and beneath these there lies the chief pasture. This *pratumSummary*, where he describes it most learnedly, for he was instructed by a Jew -- is a certain secret but universal region. One calls it the Region of Light, but to the Kabalist it is Night of the Body, a term extremely apposite and significant. It is in few words the rendezvous of all spirits, for in this place the ideas -- when they descend from the bright world to the dark one -- are incorporated. For thy better intelligence thou must know that spirits whiles they move in heaven, which is the fire-world, contract no impurities at all, according to that of Stellatus: "All," saith he, "that is above the moon is eternal and good, and there is no corruption of heavenly things." On the contrary, when spirits descend to the elemental matrix and reside in her kingdom they are blurred with the original leprosy of the matter, for here the curse raves and rules; but in heaven it is not predominant. To put an end to this point, let us hear the admirable Agrippa state it. This is he between whose lips the truth did breath and knew no other oracle.

> *The heavenly powers or spiritual essences, whiles they are in themselves, or before they are united to the Matter and are showered down from the Father of Lights through the holy intelligences and the heavens, until they come to the moon -- their influence is good, as in the first degree. But when it is received in a corrupt subject the influence also is corrupted.*

Thus he. Now, the astronomers pretend to a strange familiarity with the stars; the natural philosophers talk as much; and truly an ignorant man might well think they had been in heaven and conversed -- like Lucian's Menippus -- with Jove himself. But in good earnest these men are no more eagles than Sancho; their fancies are like his flights in the blanket and every way as short of the skies. Ask them but where the influences are received and how; bid them by fair experience prove they are present in the elements, and you have undone them. If you will trust the four corners of a figure or the three legs of a syllogism you may: this is all their evidence. Well fare the magicians, then, whose Art can demonstrate these things and put the very influences in our hands. Let is be thy study to know their Region of Light and to enter into the treasures thereof, for then thou mayst converse with spirits and understand the nature of invisible things. Then will appear unto thee the universal subject and the two mineral sperms -- white and red, of which I must speak somewhat before I make an end.

In the *PYTHAGORICAL SYNOD* which consisted of three score and ten philosophers, all Masters of the Art, it is thus written:

> *The thickness or sperm of the fire falls into the air. The thickness or spermatic part of the air, and in it the sperm of the fire, falls into the water. The thickness or spermatic substance of the water, and in it the two sperms of fire and air, fall into the earth, and there they rest and are conjoined. Therefore the earth itself is thicker than the other elements, as it openly appears and to the eye is manifest.*

Remember now what I have told thee formerly concerning the earth, what a general hospital it is, how it receives all things, not only beasts and vegetables but proud and glorious man. When death hath ruined him, his coarse parts stay here and know no other home. This earth to earth is just the doctrine of the Magi. Metals -- say they -- and all things may be reduced into that whereof they were made. They speak the very truth: it is God's own principle and He first taught it Adam. "Dust thou art and unto dust shalt thou return." But lest any man should be deceived by us, I think it just to inform you there are two reductions. One is violent and destructive, reducing bodies to their extremes; and properly it is death, or the calcination of the common chemist. The other is vital and generative, resolving bodies into their sperm or middle substance, out of which

Nature made them; for Nature makes not bodies immediately of the elements but of a sperm which she draws out of the elements. I shall explain myself to you by an example. An egg is the sperm or middle substance out of which a chick is engendered, and the moisture of it is viscous and slimy, a water and no water, for such a sperm ought to be. Suppose Doctor Coal -- I mean some broiler -- had a mind to generate something out of this egg: questionless, he would first distil it, and that with a fire able to roast the hen that laid it. Then would he calcine the *caput mortuum* and finally produce his nothing.

Here you are to observe that bodies are nothing else but sperm coagulated, and he that destroys the body by consequence destroys the sperm. Now, to reduce bodies into elements of earth and water -- as we have instanced in the egg -- is to reduce them into extremes beyond their sperm, for elements are not the sperm but the sperm is a compound made of the elements and containing in itself all that is requisite to the frame of the body. Wherefore be well advised before you distil and quarter any particular bodies, for having once separated their elements you may never generate unless you can make a sperm of those elements. But that is impossible for man to do: it is the power of God and Nature. Labour then, you that would be accounted wise, to find out our Mercury: so shall you reduce things to their mean spermatical chaos. But avoid the broiling destruction. This doctrine will spare you the vain task of distillation, if you will but remember this truth -- that sperms are not made by separation but by composition of elements; and to bring a body into sperm is not to distil it but to reduce the whole into one thick water, keeping all the parts thereof in their first natural union.

But that I may return at last to my former citation of the *Synod*. All those influences of the elements being united in one mass make our sperm or our earth -- which is earth and no earth. Take it, if thou doest know it, and divide the essences thereof, not by violence but by natural putrefaction, such as may occasion a genuine dissolution of the compound. Here thou shalt find a miraculous White Water, an influence of the moon, which is the mother of our chaos. It rules in two elements -- earth and water. After this appears the sperm or influx of the sun, which is the father of it. It is a quick celestial fire, incorporated in a thin, oleous, aerial moisture. It is incombustible, for it is fire itself and feeds upon fire; and the longer it stays in the fire the more glorious it grows. These are the two mineral sperms -- masculine and feminine. If thou dost place them both on their crystalline basis, thou hast the philosophers's flying Fire-Drake, which at the first sight of the sun breaths such a poison that nothing can stand before him. I know not what to tell thee more unless -- in the vogue of some authors -- I should give thee a phlegmatic description of the whole process, and that I can despach in two words. It is nothing else but a continual coction, the volatile essences ascending and descending, till at last they are fixed according to that excellent *prosopopoeia* of the Stone:

> *I am not dead, although my spirit's gone,*
> *For it returns, and is both off and on:*
> *Now I have life enough, now I have none.*

I suffer'd more than one could justly do;
Three souls I had and all my own, but two
Are fled: the third had almost left me too.

"What I have written, I have written." And now give me leave to look about me. Is there no powder-plot or practice?

What is become of Aristotle and Galen? Where are the scribe and pharisee, the disputers of this world? If they suffer all this and believe it too, I shall think the general conversion is come about, and I may sing:

The Virgin's sign returns, comes Saturn's reign.

But come what will come, I have once more spoken for the truth and shall for conclusion speak this much again. I have elsewhere called this subject "a celestial slime" and the middle nature. The philosophers call it the venerable nature; but amongst all the pretenders I have not yet found one that could tell me why. Hear me then, that whensoever thou dost attempt this work it may be with reverence -- not like some proud, ignorant doctor, but with less confidence and more care. This chaos hath in it the four elements, which of themselves are contrary natures; but the wisdom of God hath so placed them that their very order reconciles them. For example, air and earth are adversaries; for one is hot and moist, the other cold and dry. Now to reconcile these two God placed the water between them, which is a middle nature, or of a mean complexion between both extremes. For she is cold and moist; and as she is cold she partakes of the nature of the earth, which is cold and dry; but as she is moist she partakes of the nature of the air, which is hot and moist. Hence it is that air and earth, which are contraries in themselves, agree and embrace one another in the water, as in a middle nature which is proportionate to them both and tempers their extremities. But verily this salvo makes not up the breach, for though the water reconciles two elements like a friendly third, yet she herself fights with a fourth -- namely, with the fire. For the fire is hot and dry but the water is cold and moist, which are clear contraries. To prevent the distempers of these two God placed the air between them, which is a substance hot and moist; and as it is hot it agrees with the fire, which is hot and dry; but as it is moist it agrees with the water, which is cold and moist; so that by mediation of the air the other two extremes, namely, fire and water, are made friends and reconciled. Thus you see -- as I told you at first -- that contrary elements are united by that order and texture wherein the Wise God hath placed them.

You must now give me leave to tell you that this agreement or friendship is but partial -- a very weak love, cold and skittish. For whereas these principles agree in one quality they differ in two, as your selves may easily compute. Much need therefore have they of a more strong and able mediator to confirm and preserve their weak unity; for upon it depends the very eternity and incorruption of the creature. This blessed cement and balsam is the Spirit of the Living God, which some ignorant scribblers have called a quintessence. For this very Spirit is in the chaos and to speak plainly the fire is His throne, for in the fire He is seated, as we have sufficiently told you elsewhere. This was the reason why the Magi called the First Matter their Venerable Nature and their Blessed Stone. And in good earnest, what think you? Is it not so? This Blessed Spirit fortifies and perfects that weak disposition which the elements already have to union and peace -- for God works with Nature, not against her -- and brings them at last to a beauteous specifical fabric.

Now if you will ask me where is the soul or -- as the schoolmen abuse her -- the form all this while? What doth she do? To this I answer that she is, as all instrumentals ought to be, subject and obedient to the will of God, expecting the perfection of her body. For it is God that unites her to the body and the body to her. Soul and body are the work of God -- the one as well as the other. The soul is not the artificer of her house, for that which can make a body can also repair it and hinder death; but the soul cannot do this; it is the power and wisdom of God. In a word, to say that the soul formed the body because she is in the body is to say that the jewel made the cabinet because the jewel is in the cabinet; or that the sun made the world because the sun is in the world and cherisheth every part thereof. Learn therefore to distinguish between agents and their instruments, for if you attribute that to the creature which belongs to the Creator you bring yourselves in danger of hellfire. For God is a jealous God and will not give His glory to another. I advise my doctors therefore, both divines and physicians, not to be too rash in their censures, nor so magisterial in their discourse as I have known some professors of physic to be -- who would correct and undervalue the rest of their brethren when in truth they themselves were most shamefully ignorant. It is not ten or twelve years' experience in drugs and sops can acquaint a man with the mysteries of God's creation. "Take this and make a world" -- "Take I know not what and make a pill or clyster" -- are different receipts. We should therefore consult with our judgements before we venture our tongues and never speak but when we are sure we understand.

I knew a gentleman who, meeting with a philosopher adept, and receiving so much courtesy as to be admitted to discourse, attended his first instructions passing well. But when this magician quitted my friend's known road and began to touch and drive round the great wheel of Nature, presently my gentleman takes up the cudgels, and, urging all the authorities which in his vain judgment made for him, oppressed this noble philosopher with a most clamorous, insipid ribaldry. A goodly sight it was and worthy our imitation to see with what an admirable patience the other received him. But this errant concluded at last that lead or quicksilver must be the subject and that Nature worked upon one or both. To this the *Adeptus* replied: "Sir, it may be so at this time, but if hereafter I find Nature in those old elements where I have sometimes seen her very busy, I shall at our next meeting confute your opinion." This was all he said and it was something more than he did. Their next meeting was referred to the Greek Kalends, for he could never be seen afterwards, notwithstanding a thousand solicitations.

Such talkative, babbling people as this gentleman was, who run to every doctor for his opinion and follow like a spaniel every bird they spring, are not fit to receive these secrets. They must be serious, silent men, faithful to the Art and most faithful to their teachers. We should always remember that doctrine of Zeno: "Nature," said he, "gave us one tongue but two ears, that we might hear much and speak little." Let not any man therefore be ready to vomit forth his own shame and ignorance. Let him first examine his knowledge and especially his practice, lest upon the experience of a few violent knacks he presume to judge Nature in her very sobrieties.

To make an end: if thou dost know the First Matter, know also for certain thou hast discovered the Sancutary of Nature. There is nothing between thee and her treasures but the door. That indeed must be opened. Now if thy desire leads thee on to the practice, consider well with thyself what manner of man thou art and what it is that thou wouldst do; for it is no small matter. Thou hast resolved with thyself to be a co-operator with the Spirit of the Living God and to minister to Him in His work of generation. Have a care therefore that thou dost not hinder His work; for if thy heat exceeds the natural proportion thou hast stirred the wrath of the moist natures and they will stand up against the central fire, and the central fire against them; and there will be a terrible division in the chaos. But the sweet Spirit of Peace, the true eternal quintessence, will depart from the elements, leaving both them and thee to confusion. Neither will he apply Himself to that Matter as long as it is in thy violent, destroying hands. Take heed therefore lest thou turn partner with the devil, for it is the devil's design from the beginning of the world to set Nature at variance with herself that he may totally corrupt and destroy her. "Do not thou further his designs." I make no question but many men will laugh at this; but on my soul I speak nothing but what I have known by very good experience: therefore believe me. For my own part, it was ever my desire to bury these things in silence, or to paint them out in shadows. But I have spoken thus clearly and openly out of affection I bear to some who have deserved much more at my hands. True it is I intended sometimes to expose a greater work to the world which I promised in my *Anthroposophia*; but I have been since acquainted with that world and I found it base and unworthy; wherefore I shall keep in my first happy solitudes, for noise is nothing to me. I seek not any man's applause. If it be the will of my God to call me forth and that it may make for the honour of His Name, in that respect I may write again; for I fear not the judgement of man. But in the interim, here shall be an end.

FINIS

www.ingramcontent.com/pod-product-compliance
Lightning Source LLC
LaVergne TN
LVHW041501070426
835507LV00009B/739